CONTENTS

WHAT IS A REPTILE?

What do you think of when you think of reptiles? Do you think of lizards and snakes? One doesn't look very much like the other. Lizards have four legs and run around, sometimes very quickly. Snakes don't have any legs at all and move by slithering along the ground. Can they really be the same kind of animal?

What about crocodiles? They look a bit like giant lizards, or like the last of the dinosaurs, big and heavy with powerful jaws. They are reptiles as well.

Turtles and tortoises look very different from all these other animals. Their bodies are protected inside hard, bony shells.

▼ A tortoise can tuck its legs and head into its shell for protection if it is startled. This is a giant tortoise from the Galapagos Islands.

◀ Crocodiles have many pointed teeth, used for grasping their prey. This is a mugger crocodile.

▶ The common chameleon is a reptile with a long tongue that it uses to catch insects.

Some types of tortoise are great slow-moving land animals, while some turtles swim for great distances through the ocean. But tortoises and turtles are reptiles too.

So what is it that all these animals have in common that makes them different from all other animals? What is it that makes them reptiles? This book will help you find out.

▶ The yellow cobra from South Africa kills its prey by injecting poison with its fangs.

Did you know?

One of the heaviest reptiles is the leatherback turtle, which can weigh nearly 1600 pounds. The reptile thought to be the smallest is the dwarf gecko, which is less than $1^1/_2$ inches long.

TYPES OF REPTILE

Reptiles can be divided into four main groups. Turtles and tortoises make up the first group. There are more than 200 different types of these reptiles. Their bodies are protected inside a bony shell and they have four legs. They have no teeth but can bite with the horny beak that covers their jaws. Turtles live in or near water, whereas tortoises, sometimes called land turtles, live on land.

The next group, snakes and lizards, have long bodies and skin covered in small, overlapping **scales**. They usually have large mouths and tongues that are forked or that have a notch in the end. Most lizards have four legs, but a few don't have any legs at all. All snakes are legless, although some have remnants of tiny legs near their tails.

▲ Some snakes still have the remains of legs. You can see tiny white hind legs on this boa.

▼ There were turtles similar to this hawksbill turtle swimming in the oceans 200 million years ago.

WHAT IS A
REPTILE?

Robert Snedden

Photographs by Oxford Scientific Films

Illustrated by Adrian Lascom

Sierra Club Books for Children
San Francisco

The Sierra Club, founded in 1892 by John Muir, has devoted itself to the study and protection of the earth's scenic and ecological resources — mountains, wetlands, woodlands, wild shores and rivers, deserts and plains. The publishing program of the Sierra Club offers books to the public as a nonprofit educational service in the hope that they may enlarge the public's understanding of the Club's basic concerns. The Sierra Club has some sixty chapters in the United States and in Canada. For information about how you may participate in its programs to preserve wilderness and the quality of life, please address inquiries to Sierra Club, 85 Second Street, San Francisco, CA 94105.

First Paperback Edition 1997

First published in Great Britain in 1994 by Belitha Press Limited, London House, Great Eastern Wharf, Parkgate Road, London SW11 4NQ

Library of Congress Cataloging-in-Publication Data

Snedden, Robert;
    What is a reptile?/Robert Snedden;
photographs by Oxford Scientific Films; illustrated by Adrian Lascom.
    p.   cm.
    Includes index.
    ISBN 0-87156-493-9 (hc)
    ISBN 0-89156-930-2 (pb)
    1. Reptiles—Juvenile literature. [1. Reptiles.]
I. Lascom, Adrian, ill. II. Oxford Scientific Films.
III. Title.
QL495.5.1575
597.9—dc20   94-14422

Printed in Portugal
10 9 8 7 6 5 4 3 2 1

Editor: Carol Watson
Series designer: Frances McKay
Consultant: Dr. Jim Flegg
Educational consultant: Brenda Hart

The publisher wishes to thank the following for permission to reproduce copyrighted material:

Oxford Scientific Films and individual copyright holders on the following pages: Anthony Bannister, 15 top; Eyal Bartov, 5 right; G. I. Bernard, 16 top; Waina Cheng, 6 top; Peter Cook, 10; J. A. L. Cooke, 25 center, 26/27; Treat Davidson/Photo Researchers Inc., 25 bottom; Stephen Downer, 22; Carol Farneti/Partridge Films Ltd., 20; Michael Fogden, 21 center, 23 bottom; Mickey Gibson/Animals Animals, 11 top; W. Gregory Brown/Animals Animals, 6 bottom; Mark Hamblin, 12 top; Mark Jones, 4 bottom; Pam Kemp, cover; Michael Leach, 15 bottom, 18 bottom; Zig Leszczynski/Animals Animals, 5 left, 7 top, 9 top and bottom, 19, 25 top, 27 bottom right; Tom McHugh/Photo Researchers Inc., 28/29; S. Nagaraj, 4 top; Stan Osolinski, 8, 12 bottom, 27 top; Richard Packwood, contents page; Avril Ramage, 11 bottom; J. H. Robinson/Animals Animals, 21 top; Peter Ryley, 14; Jany Sauvanet/Photo Researchers Inc., title page; Maurice Tibbles, 24; K. G. Vock/Okapia, 16 bottom; Kim Westerskov, 7 bottom; Belinda Wright, 21 bottom, 23 top; Len Zell, 26 inset.

Front cover picture:
A parson's chameleon from Madagascar.

Title page picture: An emerald tree boa in French Guiana watches for prey.

Contents page picture: An agama lizard in Kenya keeps a lookout for intruders.

The third group, crocodiles and alligators, are very large reptiles. Their bodies have bony **plates** like armor in the skin along their backs. They have heavy jaws lined with pointed teeth, as well as long, powerful tails and short legs.

Finally there is a reptile called the tuatara. The tuatara looks very much like a lizard but is in fact a different type of reptile. Tuataras are more active in cooler temperatures than other reptiles and come out from their burrows at night to feed on insects and other small animals.

Tuataras are less than 3 feet long and have a crest of spines that runs along their backs and tails. These reptiles are found only in a few places in New Zealand.

▲ The ancestors of this crocodile, called a gavial, were alive at the time of the dinosaurs.

▼ The tuatara is the only living member of a group of reptiles that lived about 200 million years ago.

HEAT CONTROL

Birds and **mammals** are able to make their own warmth inside their bodies from the food they eat. This allows them to keep their bodies at about the same temperature all the time. A reptile can't do this. Its body temperature depends on how warm or cold its surroundings are. If a reptile gets too warm or too cold its body doesn't work properly and it is unable to move. To prevent this from happening, reptiles have a number of ways of keeping their bodies at the correct temperature.

One way of doing this is by moving from a cool place to a warm place. In the morning a reptile will come slowly out from where it has spent the night to sit in the sun.

Once it has warmed up enough it can move around looking for food. Because it is also dangerous for a reptile to overheat, those living in very hot places, such as **deserts**, move back into the shade to rest during the hottest part of the day.

Although modern reptiles are unable to make their own heat, they can control

◀ The pale skin of the desert iguana reflects the light of the sun and helps it to keep cool.

their body warmth in another way. They can adjust the amount of blood that flows through the **blood vessels** near the surface of their skin. While the reptile is trying to get warm, the surface blood vessels expand so that its blood is warmed by the sun. Later, when the day gets cooler, the vessels contract and become narrower so that less blood flows through them. This helps to keep the warmth inside the reptile's body.

Some lizards change color to adjust the warmth of their bodies. They are dark in the morning, which helps them to take in heat, and then, when they are warm enough, they become paler to **reflect** away the sun's warming rays.

◀ This alligator has come out of the water to sun itself on a log.

▲ If a crocodile gets too hot, it can cool off by opening its mouth.

REPTILE SKIN

A reptile's skin is hard and dry compared with the soft, moist skin of an **amphibian**, such as a frog. Some people think that if you touch a snake it will feel slimy, but it doesn't.

The outer section of a reptile's skin is much thicker than that of an amphibian. Many reptiles have horny scales that are formed in this section of their skin. The scales are made of **keratin**, the same substance that makes up nails, hair and feathers. They help the reptile to reduce the loss of moisture from its body. A reptile's scales are not like fish scales, which are bony.

However, some reptiles do have plates made of bone that lie beneath and support the scales in the outer skin. In turtles these plates join together forming a hard shell.

A turtle's shell is covered by a very thin layer of skin that contains **nerves** and blood vessels. Over this layer of skin there is a layer of thick, horny scales, called **scutes**. The scutes make up the outer shell that you see on turtles and tortoises. Soft-shelled turtles don't have scutes; instead, they have a thicker layer of skin over their bony shells.

▲ Crocodiles have a thick, horny skin. Bony plates on the animal's back give it greater strength and protection.

The scales of a lizard or a snake don't get bigger as the animal grows. Instead, the old scales and skin are shed every so often and are replaced by new ones.

Lizards most often shed the outer layer of skin in large flakes, but snakes usually lose theirs all at once as the old upper skin breaks away from the new layer growing beneath it.

Crocodiles and turtles don't lose their large scales or scutes. They become thicker and larger as new layers of keratin are added to them from beneath.

▲ A turtle's outer shell is made of thick, horny scales.

▼ Snakes usually shed their skins whole to reveal a new skin beneath. This is a grass snake.

TEETH AND JAWS

▼ A crocodile's jaws and teeth are suited for snapping and grasping a meal, but not for cutting.

Most lizards have teeth that are all the same shape. They are usually cone-shaped, sharp and attached directly to the jawbone, rather than being in sockets like the teeth of a mammal. Some lizards that eat other animals have particularly long teeth for grasping. Others have rows of short, sharp teeth, like those of a saw, for tearing. Plant-eating lizards may have teeth that are blunt. Many lizards just grab hold of their food, bite it and swallow it without chewing.

▶ A snake can unhinge its jaws, allowing it to swallow very large meals.

Jaw muscle

Jawbone

A snake has extra **joints** that give its skull a very loose structure. It can separate the bones of its head and jaws in order to swallow large animals that seem to be too big to fit into its mouth. Its upper and lower jaws can be separated into two halves, left and right. The two halves of the lower jaw move wide apart to make the mouth bigger. The two sides of the snake's mouth work together to pull its meal in. First the meal is held firmly by the left side of the mouth while the right-hand teeth are released and move forward to a new position. Then the left-hand teeth release their grip and move forward. And so it continues, like pulling in a rope hand over hand.

Crocodiles and alligators have long jaws lined with pointed teeth that they use to grab hold of their **prey**. They cannot chew, and their teeth don't have cutting edges. They tear off bits of their food by twisting their bodies.

Toothless turtles and tortoises can bite with their hard beaks by moving their lower jaws up and down. Like other reptiles, they don't really chew their food.

▲ The leaf-eating lizard, ▼ above, has a single sharp tooth for tearing at leaves. But most lizards, like the basilisk shown below, have two rows of sharp, pointed teeth.

GETTING AROUND

Reptiles have a variety of ways of moving, as you might imagine with animals that come in so many different shapes and sizes. Tortoises are very slow-moving animals. A typical tortoise takes only one step every two seconds. Try it yourself—it isn't very fast. Most tortoises don't need to move quickly because they eat plants and are protected by their shells.

Lizards stand with their feet far apart on either side of their bodies. They bend their bodies from side to side as they walk in order to take longer strides. Some are able to stand up and run on their hind legs.

Other types of lizard have very small legs or no legs at all. Many live in deserts and move through loose sand by waving their bodies.

Snakes don't have any legs at all. They usually move by using their muscles to throw their bodies into wavelike movements that travel backward along the body from head to tail. As its body pushes against the ground, the snake moves forward. This kind of movement is similar to the way in which eels travel through water. Snakes that live in sandy desert regions use a special sort of movement called **sidewinding**. The snake's body touches the ground in only two or three places and it swings its body forward in loops.

Crocodiles and alligators spend a lot of time in the water. They hold their legs in close to their bodies and swim by moving their huge tails from side to side. Although their legs are short, they are also able to move surprisingly quickly on land.

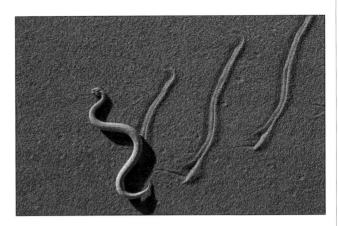

▲ Snakes of sandy deserts move by swinging their bodies forward in loops. This is called sidewinding.

Some kinds of turtle live in the open ocean and go ashore only to lay their eggs. Their feet are flattened like flippers, and the turtle moves them like the oars of a boat to propel itself through the water.

◀ Tortoises are generally slow-moving animals that don't use much energy.

▼ Some lizards, such as this flying gecko, can glide through the air for short distances to escape danger.

SIGHT AND SOUND

Sight is an important sense for almost all reptiles, helping them to detect objects around them. A reptile's eyes are always set so that it can see into the distance. If it wants to look at something nearby, it uses the muscles around the eye to change the shape of its lens. This is the part of the eye that **focuses** the light. Snakes have special muscles that force the lens forward for close vision, like focusing a camera. Many types of reptile, including some crocodiles, lizards and tortoises, can see in color.

Some reptiles have a type of third eye. It lies just under the skin on top of the head of some lizards and the tuatara. It can detect light and dark but can't make out shapes. It may be like a **light meter** that helps the reptile to judge how much time it has spent in the sun. Blind snakes, which burrow under the ground, have eyes that are covered by scales, and they can't see.

If you have ever seen a snake you may have noticed that it never closes its eyes. In fact, each of a snake's eyes is permanently covered by a transparent scale, which is the lower eyelid. These transparent eyelids protect the snake's eyes.

▲ Crocodiles have a transparent third eyelid that protects the eye while it is under water.

▼ The lower eyelid of a snake is transparent and permanently covers the eye.

Did you know?

Scientists are studying the ability of snakes to pick up vibrations traveling through the ground. This may give us advance warning of earthquakes.

Reptiles don't have outer ears, as mammals do, so it looks as if they don't have ears at all. But most reptiles have **eardrums** that are close to the surface of the skin. These pick up the **vibrations** that sound makes as it travels through the air, water or ground. The vibrations then travel along a small, thin bone to the inner ear. From there the sound messages are sent to the reptile's brain.

Snakes don't have eardrums, but they do have a thin bone positioned between the hinge of the jaw and the inner ear. Because it has no eardrums, a snake can't hear sounds traveling through the air. But it can detect vibrations traveling along the ground as they are transmitted along the bone to its inner ear. Snakes also have special vibration detectors in their skin that sense the approach of prey or **predators**.

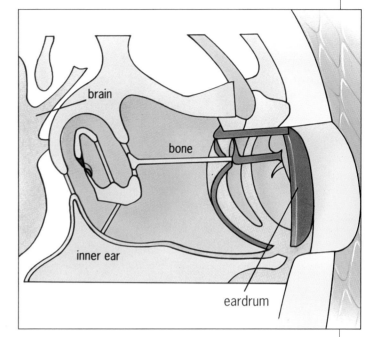

▲ A lizard's eardrums are close to the surface of the skin, where they pick up sound waves.

▶ The tuatara has a third eye in the top of its skull. This extra eye sees light and dark, but not shapes.

TASTE, SCENT AND HEAT

Sometimes it is difficult to tell whether a reptile is tasting something or smelling it. Snakes and some lizards have forked tongues that dart out of their mouths to pick up tiny particles from the air. Inside the roof of most reptiles' mouths there is a pair of holes, and inside the holes are the **Jacobson's organs**. The tips of their forked tongues are placed into or against the Jacobson's organs. These then "taste" or "smell" what is in the air. When a snake or lizard appears to be moving its tongue in and out quickly, it means that it has smelled something interesting.

Many reptiles swallow their food whole and probably don't get much chance to taste it at all. Some reptiles, however, do taste with their tongues in much the same way as we do. Chameleons catch insects with their tongues and spit them out again very quickly if they don't like the taste. They learn from bad experiences to avoid eating foul-tasting insects.

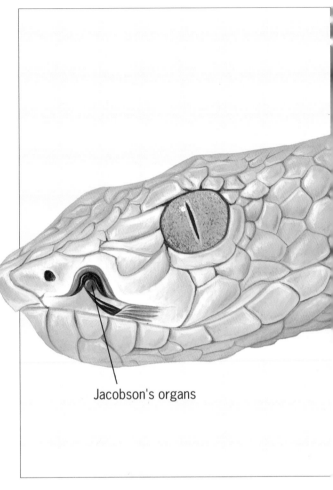

Jacobson's organs

▼ The chameleon uses its long tongue to catch its food. If this insect tastes bad, the chameleon will soon spit it out again.

▲ Snakes and lizards smell by catching scents with their tongues and transferring them to the Jacobson's organs in the roofs of their mouths.

Many snakes can sense heat by means of special detectors in their skins. Pit vipers, such as rattlesnakes, have a pair of well-developed heat detectors at the front of their heads. Using these, the snake can sense the heat from a small animal more than 6 feet away and then attack it. A pit viper's heat detection system is so sensitive that it can pick up changes in temperature of only a few thousandths of a degree.

Did you know?

A crocodile's sense of smell may be important in finding food. Crocodiles have been known to travel nearly 2 miles in order to share a meal.

▼ Pit vipers, such as this northern copperhead, have sensitive heat detectors in small pits at the front of their heads. They can find other animals in the dark by detecting the heat from their bodies.

DEFENSES

Very often the best way to avoid being attacked is to avoid being seen, and this is what many reptiles do. Some lizards and snakes are hard to see because they are **camouflaged** by having skin colors and patterns that help them to blend in with their surroundings. Chameleons in particular are known for their ability to change color. But this ability is limited to various shades of green, yellow and brown. If you put a chameleon against a background of red and blue stripes, it wouldn't be able to change to match it.

Tortoises, of course, have their tough shells to protect them. If a tortoise is disturbed, it will draw its legs and head into its shell and sit tight until the danger passes.

Many lizards can protect themselves in more active ways if they are attacked. Some will hiss at an attacker and inflate their bodies with air to look as big as possible, at the same time biting and scratching and lashing their tails. Many types of lizard have spines that make them very hard to swallow. There are also some that can break off their own tails. An animal trying to attack the lizard is often distracted by the tail thrashing about on its own, and the lizard can make its escape. Losing its tail doesn't do the lizard much harm as it can soon grow a new one.

▼ By taking on the color of the leaves around it, this flap-necked chameleon may avoid being seen and eaten by other animals.

Poisonous snakes are often brightly colored. These colors warn other animals not to try and eat them. Some other types of snake that are not poisonous mimic the colors of the poisonous ones. This tricks a predator into thinking that they are poisonous too.

Very large reptiles, such as crocodiles and alligators, are so big and powerful that no other animal would try to attack one that is fully grown.

▲ Some non-poisonous snakes mimic the colors of poisonous ones to trick other animals into avoiding them. The scarlet snake (top) is harmless, but the coral snake (bottom) is highly poisonous.

◀ The frilled lizard of Australia makes a threatening display by hissing and erecting a fringe of skin to make itself look bigger.

FEEDING

Most lizards feed on insects and other small animals. Many have large, fleshy and often sticky tongues that they can flick out to catch their food. Chameleons have particularly long tongues—sometimes as long as their bodies. Some lizards are plant eaters. The marine iguana, for example, goes into the ocean to feed on seaweed, sometimes diving 50 to 65 feet under the water. Monitor lizards will eat almost any animal that is small enough for them to handle. Monitors include the Komodo dragon, the world's biggest lizard. Komodo dragons can reach 10 feet in length and are able to eat small deer and pigs.

▲ This chameleon has caught a grasshopper with its long, sticky tongue. A chameleon's tongue can be as long as its body.

All snakes are **carnivorous.** Most of them are quite small and feed on tiny creatures such as worms and insects. Some snakes have poison **fangs** that they use to bite their prey, sometimes killing it immediately. Some snakes have fangs with grooves down which **venom** flows. Others have fangs like hollow needles and the venom comes out of the tip. Snakes with long fangs fold them back out of the way when they close their mouths.

Many non-poisonous snakes kill their prey by suffocating it. The snake wraps its coils around the animal it wants to eat and gradually tightens its hold, stopping its prey from breathing. Snakes are able to open their mouths very wide and can swallow large animals. An 18-foot-long python was once found to have swallowed a leopard more than 3 feet long.

Crocodiles and alligators often lie in wait in the water. They can float very still just under the surface, with only their eyes and nostrils showing above the water. When an animal comes to drink, the crocodile swims toward it underwater to try and grab it by surprise. It then pulls the animal down into the water and holds it there until it drowns. Crocodiles and alligators also eat fish, frogs and birds.

Turtles eat both plants and animals, biting off chunks with their hard, sharp, horny beaks. Sea turtles eat seaweed, jellyfish and small fish. Land tortoises mostly eat plants, but some also eat insects and slugs.

▲ This Australian saltwater crocodile (top left) has caught a barramundi, a type of large fish.

◀ Egg-eater snakes can stretch their mouths wide to swallow eggs that are bigger than they are.

EGGS

Reptile eggs are usually large and have shells, and they are laid on land. This is an important difference between reptiles and amphibians. Amphibians lay small eggs that have no shells, so they must lay them in water or the eggs will dry out and die. Tortoises and crocodiles lay eggs with stiff, brittle shells, like the eggs of a bird. Turtles, most lizards and snakes lay eggs with flexible, leathery shells. Inside the reptile egg is a yolk, just as there is in a bird's egg. The yolk provides nourishment for the reptile **embryo** growing inside the egg. The eggshell has

▲ Sea turtles come ashore to lay their eggs in the sand. They may lay up to a hundred at a time.

many tiny pores in its surface that let air through so that the embryo can breathe.

All female reptiles produce eggs from which their young will **hatch**. Because the eggs are laid complete with shells, they must be **fertilized** inside the female reptile's body. This is carried out by the male depositing sperm inside the female. Some types of male reptile will fight to be the one who fertilizes a female.

◄ These young hog-nosed snakes have just cut their way out of their leathery eggs.

▼ A young green turtle can be seen inside this egg.

Most female reptiles lay their eggs. Sometimes they do this in a hole in the earth like a nest. But a few types of snake and lizard produce live young by keeping their eggs inside their bodies until they hatch. This happens particularly with reptiles that live in cooler regions, as they can keep their eggs warmer inside their bodies than in any burrow they might find. Sea snakes also give birth to live young. This allows them to have their young without ever leaving the water.

Reptile eggs can't be laid in water because the growing reptile inside would not get enough **oxygen** to breathe. Turtles and crocodiles always come out of the water to lay their eggs.

Reptile embryos have a horny tip, called an egg tooth, on their snouts. This helps them to tear a small hole in the eggshell when they are ready to hatch. Often the young reptile will rest after it tears open the first hole in its shell. Some pythons remain still for several days before carrying on with hatching.

▶ American alligators make nests of rotting vegetation to keep their eggs warm.

PARENTAL CARE

Of all the reptiles, crocodiles and alligators are the ones that take best care of their young. All types of crocodile build nests for their eggs. The female American alligator builds a nest of rotting vegetation for her eggs. As the vegetation rots, its gives off heat that keeps the eggs warm. The female alligator guards the nest, and when she hears the peeping calls of the young alligators, just before they hatch, she uncovers the eggs.

The female Nile crocodile carries her young in her mouth to the water after they hatch.

She will stay nearby for several weeks and come to their help if they are in distress. All crocodiles behave in a similar way.

Tortoises and turtles generally do no more than find a suitable place to lay their eggs, cover them up and then leave them. Many turtle eggs are eaten by other animals, such as birds and crabs. Any young turtles that do manage to survive and hatch are often eaten before they can reach the sea, or before they have the chance to grow big.

▼ Inset: These newly hatched turtles have no protection against other animals.

▼ All the turtles hatch together and make their way as quickly as possible to the sea.

Like turtles, most snakes that lay eggs simply lay the eggs and then leave them to hatch on their own. But there *are* some snakes that look after their eggs. Many types of python and cobra coil around their eggs to keep them warm, although they don't look after the young once they have hatched.

A few types of lizard also look after their eggs, guarding them against other animals that might try to eat them. Just like snakes, parent lizards don't look after their young.

▼ Top right: Alligators protect their young after they hatch. This young alligator is sitting on its mother's tail.

▶ Below right: Some snakes, such as this diamondback rattlesnake, give birth to live young.

LAND INVADERS

Reptiles have played a vital part in the history of life on land. The first reptiles lived about 340 million years ago and were small animals about 8 inches long. Over the next 275 million years, reptiles became one of the most successful groups of animals there has ever been. Dinosaurs are the most famous of the ancient reptiles. For 160 million years these creatures dominated the Earth. Other large land animals, such as birds and mammals, **evolved** from reptiles.

Reptiles are better equipped to survive on land than amphibians. Reptiles have dry, scaly skins to protect them from drying out, whereas amphibians have smooth, moist skins. Reptiles lay eggs with protective shells that don't dry out on land, but amphibian eggs have a coat of jelly and are laid in water.

Young reptiles look like their parents, but young amphibians are different from adults and spend the first part of their lives in water.

Reptiles can be found all over the world except where it is too cold for them to live. They swim in the oceans and rivers, climb trees, and live in deserts and mountains.

Many types of reptile are in danger of **extinction** because people kill them for food, for their skins, or out of fear, or destroy the wild places where they live. To make sure reptiles will still share our world in the future, we must learn to take better care of these fascinating creatures and their homelands around the globe.

▼ The Komodo dragon is the world's largest lizard. It can grow to 10 feet in length and will eat animals as big as small deer and pigs.

GLOSSARY

Amphibian: A type of animal, such as a frog or newt, that lives part of its life in water and part on land.

Blood vessels: The network of tubes, called veins and arteries, that carry blood around inside the body of an animal.

Camouflage: Colors or patterns on something that help it to hide by blending in with its surroundings.

Carnivorous: Describes a creature that eats meat.

Desert: A very dry area that is often very hot.

Eardrum: The part of the ear in some types of animals that is made to vibrate by sound waves. The vibrations are then passed on to the inner ear and brain.

Embryo: A young animal growing inside an egg or inside its mother.

Evolved: Changed over a period of time.

Extinction: When an animal or a plant dies out completely so that it no longer exists.

Fangs: Long, sharp, pointed teeth. Some snakes can inject poisonous venom by biting with their fangs.

Fertilize: To join the male sperm with the female egg so that a new animal can grow from it.

Focus: To make an image sharp and well defined.

Hatch: To emerge from an egg.

Jacobson's organs: Detectors in the roof of a snake's or a lizard's mouth used to identify smells brought there by the tongue.

Joint: Part of an animal's body where bones fit together in a way that allows the bones or limbs to move or bend.

Keratin: The strong but flexible material that makes up hair, horn, nails and scales.

Light meter: A device used to measure the brightness of light.

Mammal: A type of animal that is warm-blooded and has fur or hair; female mammals provide milk to feed their young.

Nerves: Parts of an animal's body that carry messages and signals from one part of the body to another.

Oxygen: A type of gas found in air. Animals need oxygen to survive.

Plates: Thin, flat, rigid sheets; crocodiles have bony plates along their backs.

Predator: The name given to an animal that kills other animals for food.

Prey: The name given to animals that are killed and eaten by another animal.

Reflect: To bounce back something, such as light or heat, from a surface.

Scales: Thin, horny, overlapping plates that protect the skin of many reptiles.

Scutes: The bony parts of a turtle's shell.

Sidewinding: The way some desert snakes move by swinging their bodies forward in loops.

Venom: A liquid poison, injected in the bite of some snakes and spiders and in the stings of insects such as wasps.

Vibration: A rapid, to-and-fro motion.

INDEX